Keep Your Clothes On

APOSTLE JOHN N. GRAY

Keep Your Clothes On
Copyright © 2022 by John Gray
Published by Grace 4 Purpose, Publishing Co. LLC
All rights reserved. No part of this publication may be reproduced in any form or by any electronic or mechanical means, including information storage and retrieval systems, without prior permission in writing from the publisher, except by reviewers, who may quote brief passages in a review.
All scripture quotations, unless otherwise indicated, are taken from the King James Version of the Bible and other Versions. All rights reserved.
Editing by: Grace 4 Purpose, Publishing Co. LLC
ISBN: 979-8-9854834-8-2
Book cover design by Untouchable Designz and Consulting
Printed and bound in the United States of America

Table of Contents

Acknowledgments..................................Page 4

Forward..Page 5

Introduction..Page 14

Living Under God's Transformative Identity.......Page 17

God's Clothes of Favor...........................Page 28

How are we to Wear God's Clothes of Favor?.......Page 32

Why is it Dangerous to Trust God?.............Page 37

What Clothes are we Wearing?..................Page 44

God's Clothes for Our Losses....................Page 51

Wearing the Clothes of Past Reproaches..........Page 57

Obtaining the Clothes of God's Favor...........Page 62

Prayer...Page 71

About the Author...................................Page 72

Acknowledgements

My profound admiration to all those who sincerely inspired, pushed and encouraged me to finally write this book. It has been in my heart to write and publish *Keep Your Clothes On* for many years. There were many attempts to get started on this project. I started to write it, but I would never position myself to see it through. This is a raw version edition as it came into my heart. I want to express my thanks for the encouragement, prayers and support that pushed me to bring *Keep Your Clothes On* to completion.

I am forever thankful to my wife, Lady Laverne Gray, and my children who urged and pushed me to finally write the sentiments of my heart. To my very special friends who encouraged me, listened to me for hours and told me to follow my heart. I am also thankful for my church family, Bethel Restoration Center, who contributed in invaluable ways. Most of all, I thank my Lord and Savior Jesus Christ for giving me the ability to express His grace and His favor towards us in the words of this book.

Foreword

History records that we are living is one of the most troubling times of human history, while affirming what has been prophetically declared, "For men shall be lovers of their own selves, covetous, boasters, proud, blasphemers, disobedient to parents, unthankful, unholy," And as in the times of despair past, God always raises up a righteous voice. Apostle John Gray's book shines like a lighthouse in the midst of the dark seas of life." His words capture the heart of our God who desires that his people be clothed in his righteousness. 1 Corinthians 6:13 (KJV) tells us, "Now the body *is* not for fornication, but for the Lord; and the Lord for the body." Apostle Gray articulates how there is no bondage in God, only liberty! That's what the path of righteousness teaches us all until we come in the unity of faith, and of the knowledge of the son of God, unto a perfect man, unto the measure and the stature of the fulness of Christ! This book will not only clothe you, but it will also strengthen your walk and enrich your understanding!

-Apostle William Dawson
(Mt. Gilead Baptist Church-Williamsburg, VA)

Foreword

Even when you don't see Him – know that the LORD never stops working.

God is "working" in His development plan for every person. In *Keep Your Clothes On*, Apostle John Gray gives us revelation concerning His plan.

Presented here is, of sorts, a recovery strategy for the child of God to "get back up." In this manuscript, my longtime friend, Apostle Gray addresses the benefits of being under the covering and auspices of God.

In a world of violence, epidemic, pandemic, economic struggle and sin, God's presence, through strong Christians, is desperately needed. Apostle Gray challenges each of us to be those strong people of God by fighting the good fight of faith (1Timothy 6:12).

Fighting the good fight is not really fighting people, the system, our enemies or even Satan – it's fighting to stay under the anointed "garments of God"– that He might fight our battles. "Under" is where God wants us to be.

In turn, God takes the time to develop us like the Potter with the clay in the 18th chapter of Jeremiah. The Potter hides us while He transforms us–and deals with our marred and scarred lives.

Through Kingdom ideology, spiritual principles and insightful revelation, *Keep Your Clothes On* gives us hope that we can be victorious daily as well as fulfill our calling and purposeful destiny in Christ Jesus.

Let this book build you as you lay under God's divine cloth.

"Humble yourselves therefore under the mighty hand of God, that he may exalt you in due time" 1 Peter 5:6

-Bishop Lyle Dukes
(Harvest Life Changers Church-Woodbridge, Virginia)

Foreword

Beloved,
I had the privilege of reading aloud this book back to its author. What a joy to know his heart for you!
The additional insight gained leads me to say this to you, the reader of this foreword:
With a profound, yet simple presentation, the message of this offering is designed to convict, challenge, comfort and cultivate!

It will convict you if you are wearing the wrong clothes; challenge you to gratefully embrace, and comfort you as you confidently wear the clothes our God has so lovingly provided; while cultivating a practical understanding of the difference!

Therefore, you owe it to yourself and our God to read this book...OUT LOUD!

Apostle Rita Twiggs, D.D.

Foreword

The two greatest questions of Humankind is, "Who am I?" & Why am I here?", which wrestles with the issue of Identity. It is these two questions, to which God responds to Jeremiah, in Jeremiah 1:5, which emphatically states, "Before I formed thee in the belly I knew thee; and before thou camest forth out of the womb I sanctified thee, and I ordained thee a prophet unto the nations". In other words, before the egg met the sperm, and became a zygote, then an embryo and a fetus, you had an identity. Before your Mama met your Daddy…and no matter what the circumstances are that cause you to be born, you had an identity. Consider this, out of 40 to 100 million sperm released, you were the one that made it to the egg, during the time of ovulation. That means that even in the womb, you could say, "Millions didn't make it, but I was the one who did."

Every human is a tripartite being. You are a spirit-which is your God consciousness, you have a soul-which is your self-conscious, and you're in a body, which is world consciousness-through which your 5 senses operate. The essence of who you are is your spirit. It is your spirit that provides the "DNA" for your identity, which is manifest through your potential- talents, abilities and gifts, that are facilitated by your soul (psuche'-psyche). This means that you were created with everything that you need to fulfill the purpose assigned to your life.

Your "DNA" can be found in Gen. 1:26, which succinctly states, "And God said, Let us make man in our image, after our likeness: and let them have dominion over the fish of the sea, and over the fowl of the air, and over the cattle, and over all the earth, and over every creeping thing that creepeth upon the earth." It is in Gen. 1:26 that we find the three elements of the human "DNA", which represent the "clothes" that we were created to wear, even before Adam and Eve were placed in the Garden of Eden.

DNA of Destiny:

To MASTER (Dominion/Rule)- You were not designed to be under anything, but over everything. This is not about dominating people, but it's about perfecting your talents and being earnest in the calling that God has given you.

To MOBILIZE (Develop/Replenish)- You were designed to turn potential into possibilities, beyond what is seen.

To MULTIPLY (Duplicate/Reproduce)- You were created to live in an overflow of abundance and greatness.

In this book, "Keep your clothes on", my friend, Bishop John Gray provides insight and instruction, so you can wear the "clothes" that God has tailor-made for your unique identity and undeniable destiny.

To fully grasp the power of your wearing your own "clothes", you must consider the psalmist David raising celestial questions about his terrestrial existence, when he considers the superlative wonder of a finite creation made by an infinite creator, in Psalm 8:4-6,
4)What is man, that thou art mindful of him? and the son of man, that thou visitest him.
5)For thou hast made him a little lower than the angels, and hast crowned him with glory and honor
6)Thou madest him to have dominion over the works of thy hands; Thou hast put all things under his feet.
Understand, the identity of the seed is determined by the source from which it originates. The source releases the seed, so the seed can reveal the source: the oak releases an acorn, so the acorn can reveals an oak; the lion produces the cub, so the cub can reveal a lion; God releases Man, so Man can reveal God.

Because the source gives power to the seed, even after the fall of the "seed" (Adam) in the garden, the source (God) secured the future of the fruit.

That's why Paul emphatically declared in Romans 8:29-31,

29) For whom he did foreknow, he also did predestinate to be conformed to the image of his Son, that he might be the firstborn among many brethren.
30) Moreover whom he did predestinate, them he also called: and whom he called, them he also justified: and whom he justified, them he also glorified.
31) What shall we then say to these things? If God be for us, who can be against us?

There are 4 words from this scriptural text that I would like to highlight, so that you can fully grasp the grace that has secured your identity in Christ:

Foreknow- (GREEK: Proginosko)- to know in advance.

Predestinate- (GREEK: Prooridzo)- to set boundaries for what is to come.

Justified- (GREEK: Diakiosis)- to make right, judicially.

Glorified- (GREEK: Doxazo)- to give honor and put in a place of esteem.

Life has a way of attempting to "change your clothes" through trouble, trials and trauma, sometimes self-inflicted and sometimes imposed by others. However, you must remember, the "clothes" that define your identity are not external, but internal, because they come from the eternal.

1 John 3:1-2,
1)Behold, what manner of love the Father hath bestowed upon us, that we should be called the sons of God: therefore the world knoweth us not, because it knew him not. 2)Beloved, now are we the sons of God, and it doth not yet appear what we shall be: but we know that, when he shall appear, we shall be like him; for we shall see him as he is."

The poet, Ralph Waldo Emerson, said it best, "What lies behind and what lies beneath are tiny matters compared to what lies within."

Understand, the best of you is on the inside of you, so it's time for you to wear your "clothes" inside-out. This is your moment to manifest what God has placed within you, and not allow yourself to be limited by the conditions or circumstances around you.

Wear your own clothes,
Dr. Ricky Allmon
rickyallmon.org

Introduction

Under the clothes of God, we don't have to hide in fear of what we have done, but by Him we can live in faith. It is only by keeping our clothes on that we can fellowship with God. God doesn't want us to keep ourselves from Him because of what we have done, so He covers our shame and takes away the blame of sin that keeps us from His presence. By the blood of Jesus instituting the substitution of killing an animal, He covered our nakedness (sin) and allows us to have eternal life with Him. God put His clothes on us because He loves us and cares for us. He is Sovereign over all things and the purpose of His clothes on us is to create a favorable environment for us to grow past our sins, disobedience and ungodliness. When clothed by the Holy Spirit, there is a metamorphic transitioning of the phenomenological imaging of Christ. The Holy Spirit of God is transforming the mind of our Adamic nature into the mind of Christ. The real person is the unseen person, the undeveloped. We are as an embryonic, disproportionate, and dissymmetric entity; like that of chrysalis or cocoon of a caterpillar. It is fully covered with a shell, it looks as if the caterpillar is resting, but inside is where all the action is. Inside is where the caterpillar is rapidly changing within the shell of the chrysalis, and the old body parts of the caterpillar are undergoing a remarkable transformation, called metamorphosis; to become a beautiful butterfly, tissue, limbs and organs all have been changed. Under the clothes of the Spirit of God, our metamorphic change is taking place by the renewing of our minds. It is a transformation from one level of glory to another until we become a complete reproduction of the beauty of Christ.

It is in our spiritual chrysalis or the clothes of God's Spirit where we are developing to be who we were purposed to be. Yet, to the contrary, it is a despicable experience when we come to realize how defenseless, unprotected, unclothed, and uncovered we are. The exposure of the unredeemed in us robbed us of our perfect relationship with God. It was God who loved us and clothed us with His brilliant clothes of righteousness, so that we no longer live with torn pieces of the ragged clothes of reprehensible and regrettable actions, but live in the cocoon of spiritual metamorphosis.

Psalm 91:1 (KJV) says, "He that dwelleth in the secret place of the most High shall abide under the shadow of the Almighty."

It is under the shadow of His presence that introspection takes place. Here we learn that He is our refuge and fortress; in Him we are safe under the clothes of His Love.

Living Under the Clothes of God's Transformative Identity

It is a struggle for the body of Christ to keep in our possession what has been given to us by the Lord. Our enemy undeniably wants our blessings. His quest is to bombard our life and wrestle from us our possession; the things that God has given us for life and Godliness. The possession that God has allocated to us describes an action and activity of God as God. He is personified as

Omni-benevolent in perfect goodness and all our hope is a response to God's prior promises and what He has spoken before. Peradventure, I must acknowledge that God is the source and the rightful owner of everything we are capsulated with. However, there is an enemy that will steal, kill and destroy all that God wants to give us or already has given us. Satan wants to destroy our potential by stripping us of an identity that God wants to mature and bring forward. Our struggle is to keep what God has given us and know that we will not enjoy the blessing of God without being contested by our enemy. However, he knows about our concealing power of intermitted ownership in our relationship with God. The Bible says,

> *"By his divine power, God has given us everything we need for a godly life. We have received all of this by coming to know him, the one who called us to himself by means of his marvelous glory and excellence."*
> *2 Peter 1:3 (NLT)*

We are therefore not absent of any of the things that God has desired for us to have in terms of life and godliness; but we must understand that everything we presently have and will have in the future is in the timing of God. Therefore, God says that the things we have presently are the things that give us the God kind of life ability. What we have is sufficient enough to be Godly, and to make it through any situation that we are currently facing. However, we must strive to **keep our clothes on**.

Clothing as a covering is a metaphor which asseverates the unexpected, unknown, and the uninvestigated; the filth of our humanity, and the inhabitability of our Adamic nature.

Maybe it is not just our own actions that make us feel unclean on the inside; Sometimes we are on the receiving end of anthropomorphic evil induced by satanic domination of our humanistic nature.

"I know that good does not live in me-that is, in my human nature. For even though the desire to do good is in me, I am not able to do it. I don't do the good I want to do; instead, I do the evil I don't want to do. If I do what I don't

want to do, this means that I am no longer the one who does it; instead, it is the sin that lives in me."
Roman 7:18-20 (GNB)

Under God's clothes is everything becoming; the things transforming to be; the place of non-fulfillment and dissatisfaction.

Under God's clothes, there is the progressive development of conformity to Christ. "Out of sight is the me conforming to be." It is everything in evolution of what was. It is my guilt, my defilement, my unworthiness, my undiscovered self; and the fear of exposing the nakedness of an unfinished development.

> *"We must understand that everything we presently have and will have in the future is in the timing of God."*

All this aggregated shame results from the collapse of the foundation of our relationship with God. Genesis 3:7 says, "At that moment their eyes were open, and they suddenly felt shame at their nakedness. So, they sewed fig leaves together to cover themselves."

Sewing leaves together was an effort of clothing themselves to conceal their disgracefulness. Concealing our nakedness makes revealing our nakedness too vulnerable. So, we try to cover the gap between what we really are by keeping clothes over what we are not, by covering what is already revealed to the eyes of God.

"And it came to pass, when Joseph was come unto his brethren, that they stript Joseph out of his coat, his coat of many colours that was on him;

And they took him, and cast him into a pit: and the pit was empty, there was no water in it.

And they sat down to eat bread: and they lifted up their eyes and looked, and behold, a company of Ishmeelites came from Gilead with their camels bearing spicery and balm and myrrh, going to carry it down to Egypt.

And Judah said unto his brethren, What profit is it if we slay our brother, and conceal his blood?

Come, and let us sell him to the Ishmeelites, and let not our hand be upon him; for he is our brother and our flesh. And his brethren were content
Genesis 37:23-27(KJV)

This is a great story about a young man named Joseph. In Hebrew Joseph's name means may God add. The Pharaoh of Egypt also gave Joseph a name; Zepphanah Pannieh, which means revealer of secrets. In reading the story of Joseph it is apparent that he has many similarities to Christ. Throughout this story they are amplified and parallel Christ's life. We can see clearly how Joseph's humility and his exaltation mirror Christ's own humility and exaltation. They both submitted to God and allowed His will to be done. There are levels in God where we must be in total submission. God will take you into places that you don't understand; allow you to face circumstances and situations beyond your control; and by divine providence take you into a place beyond comprehension. There you will find yourself in unfamiliar territory that you did nothing to get there. Until you can humble yourself and have faith in places you don't understand, you will never be able to advance to great places of exaltation. There must be a certain level of humbleness before we get to greatness. Christ demonstrated that, and so did Joseph.

Joseph was the faithful and favored son. He was devoted to his father. He did not allow himself to hide the sins of others, nor did he participate in the ungodly activities, as his brothers did. He had no problem in exposing his brothers. He had eleven stepbrothers, one stepsister, and a baby brother named Benjamin. Joseph was the son of his father's old age. When Rachel, who he loved dearly, died. Joseph finds himself in a place of favor that he had nothing to do with. It becomes apparent that his father Jacob didn't learn his lesson. His history with his own mother and father in terms of partiality with his brother Esau should have been enough. However, Jacob gives the son of his old age, the child of his beloved Rachel, the favored one, a coat of many colors, and gives the others nothing.

This coat represents superiority, greatness, favor, acceptance, and his inevitability to rule. It speaks to a double portion of God's anointing. It came down long to his ankles and out past his wrists. Wearing the coat gave Joseph stature and presence and caused envy and hatred among his brothers. The coat expresses delight and pleasure in the son of Rachel, but none of such in all the sons of Leah.

God longs to give us a mantle of favor just like Jacob had given to Joseph. A mantle of favor says that God wants to envelop us in His delight. He wants us to be so captured by His covering that we believe whatever we desire when we pray can become ours. He wants His mantle to cover our lives so that whatever comes against us, we will know that we are protected by the hand of God. Like Joseph was favored, God also wants us to be favored.

Could this be the reason for God clothing Adam and Eve with animal skin to apron their state of guilt which was reflected in their anthropomorphic nature? They were like us before the blood of Jesus covered us. We were naked and ashamed. God perhaps gives us the clothes of favor not to minimize our internal weakness; but to innately with introspection help us confess that we are not what we should be.

We keep our clothes on with all human determination as a witness to the glory of God that we know we have weaknesses. However, when our clothes are taken off, it reveals the shame that God hasn't finished completing in our lives.

Keeping our clothes on as it relates to God's plan for our life and our life's circumstances makes people think about what is under them. It is the enshrouded cabalistic, supernatural clothes of God's Spirit redefining our spirit that directs people's attention to what could be under them. It is the unfinished work of Jesus Christ beholding the favor and glory of Jesus the Christ. It is the testimony that one day God will make us what we should be.

"For those God foreknew he also predestined to be conformed to the image of his Son, that he might be the firstborn among many brothers and sisters."
Roman 8:29 (NIV)

In Memory of My Daughter- Melissa Woodson
"A woman who wore God's clothes of favor!"

God's Clothes of Favor?

There is something about favor; favor gives us access in doors that we wouldn't normally have. Favor will take you places that you couldn't get into by yourself. Favor means that someone delights in what you do, and how you carry yourself. It is also favor that will cause people to bless you when you don't even think you deserve it. There are doors that are opened simply because you are favored. It can get us into places; it will expose us to people; and it positions us in places where God can use us. God is trying to position His people in a place where we can be used, but we must understand that we must learn how to wear favor. We desperately need God's favor to cover the flaws in the fabric of our life. God gives to us His favor to cover some things in our lives, until we can figure out what things we don't want in our lives. It is the mutation of favor in which one circumstance is replaced by another of the same class.

> *"There are doors that are opened simply because you are favored."*

I believe that God's transcendent purpose is to mutate His people for each of us to bring Him glory. He uses His Spirit and His Word which clothe us to accomplish this.

I had the opportunity to visit a friend of 14 years I had not seen in many years. It was while participating in a commemorative walk for my oldest daughter, Melissa who died in 2012 at 46 years old from complications of Multiple Sclerosis, I was told that my friend wanted me to visit him. After walking three miles in memory of my daughter in the hot sun going up and down hills, I was tired and exhausted from the heat and the walk. When the walk was concluded I headed over to my friend's house, I was amazed to see him sitting there with his legs amputated above his knees. I noticed that one of them was freshly amputated. Something inside of me felt strange as I looked at the fresh punctured holes from staples that helped hold the flesh of his legs together. I began to realize how very blessed I am and how good God is in preserving us. As I listened to him tell me about the challenges he had faced in his life, the loss of his wife who he loves so dearly, and then losing his legs, he became angry with God and with the predicament his life was in.

Circumstances were trying to strip off his spiritual clothes and expose the hurt, pain and even his trust in

God. There is that tenacious battle for many of us to wear clothes that don't seem to fit anymore. Life sometimes seems to give very little reason to keep our clothes on, when there is so much pain from the past and the present.

There are painful situations that sometimes make us seemingly feel as though God's clothing of us is not impenetrable enough to prevent the tenacious inflicting difficulties of this world.

There are times when we feel like giving in to defeat, and our desperate place for deliverance. It is in these moments that we are reassured that the Holy Spirit has clothed us under His Divine Covering.

"Consider it all joy, my brothers and sisters, when you encounter various trials, knowing that the testing of your faith produces endurance. And let endurance have its perfect result, so that you may be perfect and complete, lacking nothing."
James 1:2-4(NASB)

How Are We to Wear God's Clothes of Favor?

Wearing the clothes of God's favor is a witness both to our purpose and present failure and to our future glory. They testify to the exhibition between what we are and what we should be.

We must learn how to put it on, how to protect it and we must realize that it is special clothing. When you have something special you must guard it because someone will want what you have. If you didn't have anything special that the devil wants, he wouldn't be trying to take what you have. The devil realizes that God has put something in you of deliberation or consideration with reference to action that has value in itself. God doesn't want the enemy to steal our life. The enemy knows our latent potentiality or our capability of becoming identifiable with the favor of Christ. So, he causes physical encounters, trying to disrobe what God is covering to bring to maturity. Our quest and battles are simply because we are wearing the favor of God. God is blessing us in areas where we are getting double for our trouble.

Joseph's eleven brothers got angry because when Joseph got blessed with two blessings, they only got blessed with one. Joseph with his other brothers had the love of a human father, but the love the father had for his son was an external reference of favor. However, Joseph was also wearing the clothes of the favor of God. Moving in the favor of God brings abundant blessings. They not only extended to external charisma, or God's divine conferred gift or power, but also the supernatural blessings of being protected by the clothing of the Holy Spirit.

Problems arise when others see the blessings. The evidence of our blessings can put us in dangerous environments. People will notice and wonder to themselves, "Why is God blessing them more, we're living in the same house, eating at the same table, we both have the same daddy, but my blessing is considerably less?" Something starts to happen on the inside that causes people to feel inferior and inadequate. It will seem to appear that the father has favoritism, but it's not about favoritism, it is about the relationship you have with your father. What God desires is a relationship. The father will bless the one who is faithful, and not the one who isn't.

Deuteronomy 7:9-10 (NASB) says, "Know therefore that the LORD your God, He is God, the faithful God, who keeps His covenant and His faithfulness to a thousand generations for those who love Him and keep His commandments; [10] *but He repays those who hate Him to their faces, to eliminate them; He will not hesitate toward him who hates Him, He will repay him to his face"*

When God told Samuel in 1 Samuel 16:11, to go to Jesse's house because He had chosen one of his sons to be king, seven of Jesse's sons passed before Samuel with different identifiable identities. None of them were wearing clothes that looked like the heart of God. David, although he wasn't clothed with an external identifiable identity, was clothed with the heart of God's favor.

So, we must learn how to wear the clothes of God's favor. We must be careful of how blessed folk know we really are. It's not just the people you don't know, but it is also the people you see systematically, even (church) folk. We must be careful with our blessings, with our favor, and with our clothes of God's favor.

*"For You, O LORD, will bless the righteous;
With favor You will surround him as with a shield."
Psalm 5:12* (NKJV)

With God's clothe of favor, we can be absolutely safe from all the incoming projectiles and missiles of the enemy and no matter what difficulties or challenges come upon us, when we are under the covering of the Lord's favor, He encircles us against the pressures of life.

God clothed us with His favor as a guarantee of His presence, grace, mercy, and His power to accomplish His predestinated purpose in and through our lives.

God spreads Himself over us like a hen her chicks; covering us while developing us to manifest His predestined will in our lives.

Psalm 91:4 (NKJV), *declares, "He shall cover you with His feathers, And under His wings you shall take refuge."*

When we are clothed with His covering, we don't have to fear the turmoil of inadequacy, insufficiency, or our inability because God is shielding us while He is growing us into a more mature person.

> "With God's clothe, we can be absolutely safe from all the incoming projectiles and missiles of the enemy."

Why Is It Dangerous to Trust God?

Trusting God leaves us vulnerable, exposed and even discoverable. Being vulnerable to God means He has the propensity to expose the rationalized personal strength that we so carefully conceal. The danger of trusting God is knowing His impeccable power, and to be vulnerable to Him is to be capable of being wounded, physically, emotionally, and spiritually.

Our vulnerability is knowing that God knows everything about us others do not know. Therefore, we must trust Him knowing that He has the power to expose what no one else knows.

Trusting our vulnerability to God in the vulnerable places in our life is less vulnerable than standing in places of susceptibility and weaknesses.

It is the cover of the clothes of God's Spirit that harborages our shame and allows us to be drawn near to God in full assurance of His care.

It is difficult for many of us to expose our personal struggles. We would much rather exhibit our asseveration of strength than acknowledge our weaknesses, even though God can be glorified in our weakness.

Because of unrevealed humanistic immorality and insufficiencies, we still lack viscosity or a degree of density in our vulnerability before God. Yet, under the clothes of God's grace and favor, He already knows everything about us.

> *1 John 3:20 (NLT) says, "Even if we feel guilty, God is greater than our feelings, and he knows everything."*

There are times when we are filled with apprehension concerning the mutations and the challenges God has for us; or what He might divulge about our character. Our prayer is that while we are in God's protective custody, He will empower us in such a no-nonsense way that our vulnerability will be turned into victory.

Charles Spurgeon said, "To trust God in the light is nothing, but to trust Him in the dark, that is faith." It is scary to trust God in our vulnerable places, but who do you trust when others don't see what we see in ourselves? And what we see in ourselves we know God sees; therefore, we are constrained to trust that what He sees will only be revealed after transformation.

Trusting in God under the clothes of transition is the ability to obey God as He walks us forward into new seasonal developments. Trust in God is therefore indispensable. Giving Him our hearts and not our head is paramount, because we cannot live in both places.

Many times, there is the propensity to not trust God in the transition, knowing that He knows all. So, instead of running from beneath the clothes of the Holy Spirit, let us remain incubated in the spiritual truths of God Word, knowing that He is our Keeper.

> *"The Lord is faithful to His Words and kind in all His works. The Lord upholds all who are falling and raises up all who are bowed down. The eyes of all looks to you, and you give them their food in due season. You open your hands; you satisfy the desires of every living thing. The Lord is righteous in all His ways and kind in all His works. The Lord is near to all who call on him in truth. He fulfills the desire of those who fear him; He also hears their cry and saves them. The Lord preserves all who love him, but all the wicked He will destroy. My mouth will speak the praises of the Lord, and let all flesh bless his holy name forever and ever.*
> *Psalm 145:13-21 (NIV)*

What a privilege to know that nothing about us can shock God. He knew our thoughts, actions, fears, and choices before we were ever born. His omniscience helps us to know that our life does not depend on our performance, but on the assurance that God is recreating us to fulfill His purpose.

Knowing His love for us takes away our fear of premature vulnerability, because we were created in Him before the world was created. We existed in the mind of God and in the sight of God. He knew who we would be and the direction our life would take. Under the clothes of His Spirit, He is securing every tiny detail of our lives; this is how we are transformed into the miracle of all He predestined us to be.

> Ephesians 1:4-5 (ESV) *"Even as he chose us in him before the foundation of the world, that we should be holy and blameless before him. In love he predestined us for adoption to himself as sons through Jesus Christ, according to the purpose of his will."*

> *"He is securing every tiny detail of our lives; this is how we are transformed into the miracle of all He predestined us to be."*

One of the difficulties in trusting God is our ability to understand God. As we live with the hurt and dysfunction that we encounter day in and day out, it is hard to figure out who our enemies are, and who we can trust. It is in this season we are tempted to believe that when life is hard, it's somehow an indication that God has abandoned us; or that He is untrustworthy. Yet in this season, God is fighting for us in the background of our battles, and this shows us exactly how to trust God in our vulnerable times of life.

Yes, we can trust God in all things, and for all things, even though sometimes trusting Him completely can be tough.

> Psalm 62:6 (NKJV) says, "He only is my rock and my salvation; He is my defense; I shall not be moved."

God stands as a bodyguard to everyone who believes in Him, and trusts in Him. The question is, where would we be if we didn't have a heart that trusts God? In our striving to become fully developed under the clothes of

God's spirit, life's circumstances can be very difficult, and could cause us to take our eyes off the Lord.

The best way forward is to live in expectancy and with a trusting heart in God. Trusting that what seems impossible, even in our vulnerable condition, is possible with God. Sometimes we are not sure where this life path is taking us, but with a heart that trusts God, we know that God will take us from paths of wondering to paths of wonderful.

What Clothes Are We Wearing?

We must realize that we all figuratively wear God. Galatians 3:27 NIV says, "And all who have been united with Christ in baptism have put on Christ, like putting on new clothes." Colossians 1:27 tells us that God has chosen to make known among the Gentiles the glorious riches of this mystery, which is Christ in you, the hope of glory. However, there are times when the clothes we wear prevaricate (misrepresent) God's Spirit and do not seem to indicate who we really are in God. So, let's look at this question: how do you keep clothes on your heart and pull off the clothes of your head?

Roman 7:21 (NIV) says, "So I find this law at work: Although I want to do good, evil is right there with me. (22) For in my inner being I delight in God's law; (23) but I see another law at work in me, waging war against the law of my mind and making me a prisoner of the law of sin at work within me."

It's under the clothes of God's favor He brings regeneration to our hearts. The old man's heart is dark, hard, and corrupt. Under the clothes of God grace, He is making us a new heart with power to control the things that are in our head that are not identifiable of God.

The heart is God's dwelling place where He develops His spoken Word. It is a discourse of developing the carnal man into the super-finite personality of the incarnate Son of God. It is the chrestologia or "useful discourse" where the Word is used to regenerate the heart for a place where the head can find renewal.

Ezekiel 36:26-27 (NLT) "And I will give you a new heart, and I will put a new spirit in you. I will take out your stony, stubborn heart and give you a tender, responsive heart. And I will put My Spirit in you so that you will follow My decrees and be careful to obey My regulations."

God offered Jesus as a heart fixer and a mind regulator.

It is the work of the Holy Spirit to develop the characteristics of Christ while under the cover of His anointing. He is taking off the ugly clothes of our selfishness, hate, guilt and shame; and wrapping us with the beautiful clothes of His incredible character.

The Holy Spirit is teaching us to wear the clothes of compassion, kindness, humility, gentleness, and patience. (Colossians 3:12)

Whatever you might be going through, do not take your clothes off, because God is dressing you with His anointing. He has you in His recovery room from your painful inflicting battle; but God has given you a special apparatus to recover you from life's anesthesia of postoperative conditions. God is dressing you to expose you, and where He has brought you from is about to give revelation of God's Divine recovery. What He has developed in you is about to be revealed, and what you are wearing is going to give glory to God. The clothes you are wearing are going to give you the power to walk away from your situation. The vulnerability of your past cannot stop the promise of your victory, because the clothes you wear are the clothes you have been empowered with from the anointing of God.

Revelation 3:18 (NKJV) says, "I counsel you to buy from Me gold refined in the fire, that you may be rich; and white garments, that you may be clothed, that the shame of your nakedness may not be revealed; and anoint your eyes with eye salve, that you may see."

In God's eye, we are naked while covered with His clothes. Wearing God's clothes is not always about what is seen as much as it is about what God is saying. He doesn't see us as a mistake, or a flaw characterized by imperfection: but He makes provisions to cover us as He cut the pattern for our destiny. In eternity past God saw what we looked like in eternity future.

From the words of Dr. Ralph Kuyper, "The whole Christian life is simply becoming what you are. This is who you are, and this is how you are to live, living up to who you are." God's systematization of us is for the glorious hope of the future. Before we were born, every gift, and every anointing was emulated from the clothes of God's Spirit to model in this present moment.

He blessed us with all spiritual blessing.
He chose us in Him before the foundation of the world.
He made us to be holy, to be blameless, in love.
He even predestined us.
He circumscribed our living to our identity, because we are called to the glorious hope of the future.

The clothes God dresses us with have their identity in Jesus: Compassion, Kindness, Humility, Gentleness, Patience, bearing with one another and Forgiveness.

Colossians 3:12-14 (NASB) says, "So, as those who have been chosen of God, holy and beloved, put on a heart of compassion, kindness, humility, gentleness, and patience.[12]

Bearing with one another, and forgiving each other, whoever has a complaint against anyone; just as the Lord forgives you, so must you also do.[13] In addition to all these things put on love, which is the perfect bond of unity.[14]

There can be no living unless there is a principle for it. There can be no lifestyle unless there is a theology at the bottom of it. When God called us in eternity past, He preordained and prearranged our life to live out what is already in us.

Romans 8:30 (NASB) says, "And these whom He predestined, He also called; and these whom He called, He also justified, and these whom He justified; He also glorified."

Although we are clothed with God's preordination and prearrangement for our lives, we will still have setbacks, disappointments and discouragements as God grows a Christlike character in us.

We have an audacious opportunity to dress ourselves with the spiritual clothes of God by putting on the fruit of the Spirit. So let us wear God's finest; the new spiritual clothes of Christ, and no longer the clothes of the old self; but the new clothes of God's favor.

> *"Before we were born, every gift, and every anointing was emulated from the clothes of God's Spirit to model in this present moment."*

God's Clothes for Our Losses

It is the old man of the heart who is trying to pull off the clothes of The Holy Spirit by showing you all the things you have lost. You are being troubled emotionally from the things that have been taken from you. That's why you are so demoralized and unable to give God a true praise. You don't know how to deal with the pain of what the enemy has taken from you; the loss of your husband, your wife, or a close friend. He has got a hold of your children and put them on drugs. You are now feeling like the tinman and demonstrating your loss by your personal emotional outbreaks.

Maybe your prayers haven't been answered yet. Maybe you feel they have been hindered, and for some reason God hasn't shown up yet. Your heart feels like it is beginning to fail and malfunction. It is the enemy trying to molest and interfere in your life and rob you of your blessing, while God is developing you under the covering of the Holy Spirit.

Romans 5:5 (NIV) says, "And hope does not put to shame, because God's love has been poured out into our hearts through the Holy Spirit, who has been given to us."

Even while in the process of development, God tells us He loves us. He is saying that we matter to Him; we are persons of worth; and we are valuable to Him.

It is amazing to know that God knows everything there is to know about us, and still loves us. He knows that we are sinners, yet He forgives. He knows we carry with us our genetic developmental infections, yet He heals. We are sometimes ungrateful for the good gifts He gives us, yet He gives them anyway.

If we ever wonder whether God loves us, just look at the red coat covered with His blood from the cross.-The cross is God's way of saying, *"I love you this much,"* with the clothes of His Spirit and with His out-stretched arms, His blood screams, *"I love you."*

It is only the clothes that God provides for us that help us to handle the excruciating, devastating losses so many have experienced in life. Yet we can see them as trials in the midst of divine development. Even in times of loss, we can see God's coat of favor covering us every minute and every hour of every day. We must keep on the clothes of God's favor and be assured that even in the depths of our loss, God's grace will always be there redeveloping everything we have lost. God is a God of restoration, and His cover of favor will never be insufficient for our needs, nor there ever be a shortage of His love.

Isaiah 54:10 (NLT) says, "For the mountains may move and the hills disappear, but even then my faithful love for you will remain. My covenant of blessing will never be broken, says the LORD, who has mercy on you."

Under the concealment of God's love, He will keep you strong, Even in the midst devastating loss, God is releasing His love for greater things in your life. He wants you to have a deep assurance that His plan is to cover and strengthen you in every place no matter what the circumstances. His strength is perfect in our weakest moments. It is God's purpose to make you strong. In fac, He is the One who gives power and strength to His people. (Psalm 68:35-NKJV) We are even commanded to *"Be strong in the Lord, and in the power of His might!"* Ephesians 6:10 (NKJV) We realize that reality tells us that we are going to experience trials in this life; but if we go through them while under the clothes of God's strength, we can respond to them with a different level of strength. No trial has the ability to be bigger than God.

He is bigger than all our problems. During extravagant enormous difficulties, God wants you to be strong. You must have an unshakeable confidence that God's purpose is intended to make you strong in Him. When you are faced with situations of loss which you don't understand; or when you encounter obstacles, difficulties, or painful situations which you were not expecting; it is easy to lose sight of God's purpose. Don't miss God's purpose even in your loss. Maybe you are encountering some weakness, stress or even struggling with depression? It is in those moments we ask God to help us keep our clothes on: to clothe you with His strength to endure; to clothe you to go on when you are filled with doubt and fear; to clothe you to trust when you feel like you can't take another step; and to clothe you to rejoice even when you are sad, because God will give you the strength to keep His clothes on you.

In this world there seems to be an abundance of insanity, instability, and insecurity. However, in the midst of it all; in the midst of all of our losses; God is assuring us that He is with us, covering us with the cloud of His glory!

Psalm 46:5-7 (NLT) says, "God dwells in that city; it cannot be destroyed. From the very break of day, God will protect it. The nations are in chaos, and their kingdoms crumble! God's voice thunders, and the earth melts! The LORD of Heaven's Armies is here among us; the God of Israel is our fortress."

"Don't miss God's purpose even in your loss."

Wearing The Clothes of Past Reproaches

Satan uses his deception to make us feel disgraced, and he uses his deception to make us feel useless. He uses the shame of the things we have done, and he tries to make us feel guilty of those things even if God has forgiven us of them. God has forgiven us, but we haven't forgiven ourselves. We walk around feeling disgraced, unworthy, and nasty for the things we've done. Even though God said those things were over, "go on," we are walking around with clothes that display and indicate that we don't feel good about ourselves, so we can't help anyone else. The enemy will keep you on a guilt trip so you can't help anyone else on their trip out of their issues because all you can see is you and your shame. It is not about us, it is about God! For if God has forgiven us, we must shake these deceptions off and praise God for the victory. We don't see ourselves as worthy, but God has made us worthy. He knew that we would make mistakes before we were conceived in our mother's womb, but He is able to forgive us. We must go on and stay clothed with the Holy Spirit's power.

There is no bondage in God's clothes, only liberty. God is the only one that can clothe us in His favor. Just because we wear the covering of His favor doesn't mean that we won't be attacked. Just because we're wrapped up in the favor and delight of God doesn't mean that we won't be tempted. We are the ones who will be attacked. We are the ones with the anointing. The enemy comes to pull off our anointing that he might expose what God is transforming.

John 10:10 (KJV) "The thief cometh not, but for to steal, and to kill, and to destroy: I am come that they might have life, and that they might have it more abundantly."

> "There is no bondage in Gods clothe, only liberty."

When Joseph's brothers saw his coat of favor, they literally tore it off of him. They became so enraged when they saw the delight, favor and anointing on him. They wanted to strip him of it. Likewise, Satan wants to strip us of everything that looks like God, and everything God said is for us. But the promise of God itself brings great relief to those of us who are clothed with the covering of God's spirit. This renewing promise of God keeps us from sinking into despair. God is saying to us that everything the enemy destroyed He made, and He can rebuild it again for His glory.

God is the maker and creator of this promise; He has laid the "scheme," the systematic plan for a course of action, and He will establish it!

When life's pandemics come as storms raging all around us, we are kept safe; hidden beneath the shield of God's favor and love. His love is like a shield around us as He spreads His protection over us.

It was Abram who heard a word from God in his reproach in a vision. God said to Abram, *"I am your shield, your very great reward."* Genesis 15:1 (NIV) The word shield is from the word "magen" which is the word "benefactor," or "suzerain" meaning, to control over a dependent state. Whatever our state might be, God is our benefactor, supporter, protector, and our exceedingly great reward. Even while wearing the clothes of our past reproach, it is through Jesus being the life of God, who has merited this glorious reward for us. His glory is imparted not impaired; it is a distribution without diminution.

> Paul said in *2 Corinthians 12:7-9 (NASB)*
> *"Because of the extraordinary greatness of the revelations, for this reason, to keep me from exalting myself, there was given to me a thorn in the flesh, a messenger of Satan to torment me-to keep me from exalting myself![7] Concerning this I pleaded with the Lord three times that it might leave me.[8] And He has said to me, "My grace is sufficient for you, for power is perfected in weakness." Most gladly, therefore, I will rater boast about my weaknesses, so that the power of Christ may dwell in me.[9]"*

For all the clothes of reproach, disapproval, and disappointments we are wearing, the Lord says to us as He did Paul, "My grace is sufficient for you, for my power is made perfect in weakness."

We pray for many things with fervor and faith to remove some of the reproach of disappointments, hurt or some un-desirable things regarding our welfare which are not answered in the way we thought.

There are times when the grace that will be imparted if the clothes of reproach are not removed, will be of greater value to a person than if there was a direct answer to his prayer. And it might not be for the good of a person who prays that the exact thing should be granted. But when enduring reproaches, we must make the affirmation, "I am weak enough to be strong." Our clothes of reproach are not just the work of Satan, but the work of God. Satan tries to use them as destructive design to destroy our reformation that God has for us; but our reproaches are expedited by God for our good. God's reformation of us even while wearing clothes of reproach is to make us a "showcase" for Jesus' power.

If it is in God's will to show us the perfection of His Son's power in our reproach, instead of our escape from it, then He knows best. The deepest need we have in wearing our clothes of reproach and adversity is not "quick relief," but the well-grounded confidence that God's reforming in us is part of the greatest purpose of God for us.

Obtaining the Clothes of God's Favor?

God's favor comes first by His connection with us as a covering over us only through Jesus Christ our Lord.

God's favor is His grace as a divine kindness and compassion towards those who need it and are undeserving. It is God's favor or grace that He gives us while under the clothing of His Spirit; giving us the ability to manifest something which is eugenically impossible for us to do.

Another way to obtain favor is to explore God's wisdom. *Proverbs 8:35 (NLT)says, "For whoever finds me finds life and receives favor from the Lord."* Under the clothe of God's favor, God is changing our action and attitude. The Holy Spirit is working to open doors that we can walk through, each one of them clothe with the favor of God, because God surrounds us with His favor.

Psalm 5:12 (NLT) says, "For you bless the godly, O Lord; you surround them with your love."

God always favors what He forms. Paul said, *"For it is by grace you have been saved through faith-and this is not from yourselves; it is the gift of God." Ephesians 2:8 (NIV)*

Today, God wants to cover you with the coat of His grace. Whatever life's challenges are, never take off the clothing of His grace.

Under the clothe of God's grace, His favor is working nonstop on your behalf. Under His grace He will pour out more favor on you moment by moment every day of your life. He mutates our circumstances by the influence of His favor.

In these unprecedented times we need to always see ourselves wrapped in the clothes of the favor of God's Spirit, and always, *"Keep Your Clothes On."* Note: Remember that the designer labeled clothes is someone else's dream. God knows everything that is to take place in our lives; even our most intermate desires and dreams. There is nothing in our thoughts that is out of God's sight.

Hebrews 4:13 (NIV) says, "Nothing in all creation is hidden from God's sight."

Obtaining God's favor under the clothes of His guardianship helps us to see what God sees in us; which is the transitioning of predestinated purpose. But if we refuse to acknowledge our human imperfections and vindicate that we have no sin, we deceive ourselves and the truth is not in us. Obtaining the coat of God's favor acknowledges the fact that He knows everything about us, and He still loves us. Who would love us if they knew everything that God knows about us? Only God will love us with unconditional love while conditioning us to love. Obtaining God's clothes of favor is simply allowing Him to do His work in us. For God to work in us we must keep His clothes on while He is applying His Divine operation in our heart. God is working on us to be sovereign in us, in the inner man of the heart, bringing our will to be conformed to His will.

"For it is God which worketh in you both to will and to do of his good pleasure." Philippians 2:13 (KJV)

> *"Obtaining God's clothes of favor is simply allowing Him to do His work in us."*

Obtaining God's clothes of favor implies that God has His eyes on us. If something tries to stop the work that He is doing in us, He will wrap us in His clothes of favor. Obtaining God's clothes of favor is an incredible blessing from the Lord. God's covering favor is one of the greatest things you can have upon you. It is the supernatural covering of God over our lives. With the clothes of God over us nothing can keep us down.

Keeping our clothes on will bring us out of our difficulties and turn our adversities around for good.

Keeping our clothes on is God's favor that moves us from our present situation into the destiny that God has for us. God is watching the clothes He puts on us to fulfill His Word in our life. Whatever He says He fulfills. In fact, He who has begun a good work in us, will be faithful to complete it. The clothes of His favor are causing us to re-enter our promised possession, His favor can change our "I am," or what we perceive ourselves to be, to what we were created to be.

So, what would our life be like if we were "surrounded" all day and every day, by the clothes of God's favor? How would our life be changed if doors are opened for us, and we go through each door with the clothes of God's favor? How would we act if we knew beyond a doubt that our success lies in the move of God just ahead of us?

God's favor is multiplied in our lives when we believe that the favor of God that is on Jesus is with us. We should always see ourselves wrapped in God's favor, surrounded like a shield. John Piper said, "God is most in us when we are most satisfied in Him." We can be joyful even when under attack because the shield of God's favor surrounds us. There will be doors waiting to be opened that only God's clothes of favor can unlock.

As doors to the clothes of God's favor opens, we decree by which events are foreordained in, *Psalm 5:12 (NIV) "Surely, LORD, you bless the righteous; you surround them with your favor as with a shield."* Whatever challenging or circumstances life may bring, we must *"Keep Our Clothes On!"*

Although God surrounds us with compassion, some of us have worn labels in our clothes so long they seem stitched into the fiber of our being. Sometimes it seems as though we like our labels because they are comfortable, and we know how they work, and they seem to provide us with some security. What labels, what covering are we wearing today?

We need to de-mask old identities and put on the clothes of God's favor. It is the clothes of His favor that will connect us to our destiny and to His supernatural grace. Obtaining God's favor is obtaining God's goodness. Life might be problematic and circumstances difficult, yet we are to look for the favor of God in every situation; because there is a purpose God wants to fulfill at the end, only if we can keep our clothes on. Like Joseph, God was in all his trials, and he declared at the end of his life to his brothers; the ones who tried to kill him, "You intended to harm me, but God intended it for good."

Finally, we must keep the favor of God's clothes on us to accomplish the sovereignty of God's will and finish the purpose of God in our lives.

In Isaiah 66:2 (ESV) God said, *"All these things my hand has made, and so all these things came to be, declares the LORD. But this is the one to whom I will look: he who is humble and contrite in spirit and trembles at my word."*

Gracious God our father we come today to thank you for the many things you have already done in our lives. You have kept us from many dangers', toils and snares of our enemy. We pray that the blood of Jesus would cover us and protect us from the enemy that surrounds us. We pray that you would keep our hearts right before you and that we forever be in the posture of repentance. Lord guard our paths and help us not to falter or fall out of love with You, but keep us under your wings, and remind us daily that we are accountable to an Almighty God.

Amen.

About The Author

Apostle John N. Gray is the senior pastor of Bethel Restoration Center (BRC) located in the beautiful city of Williamsburg, VA. For years, Apostle Gray served faithfully under his spiritual-father and former pastor, the late Bishop Christal T. Hairston, Sr.

After receiving the call to pastor, Apostle Gray began his ministry with a congregation of eight people. From this conception, a building for ministry was born in 1984-the edifice held approximately 150 people.

In 1998, God commanded Apostle Gray to build again and out of his obedience, Bethel Restoration Center was manifested-an edifice that seats 800 people and is yet progressing!

In July of 2001, Apostle Gray was consecrated into the Bishopric and in 2006, he was appointed to the Executive Board of Bishops of Bible Way Church of Our Lord Jesus Christ Worldwide. In July of 2018, Apostle Gray was consecrated as the 2nd Vice Presiding Bishop and affirmed to the office of Apostle of the International Bible Way Church of Jesus Christ, Inc. Yet again, in 2019, through his obedience to God, Apostle Gray was elevated within the same organization to be the 1st Vice Presiding Bishop, where he continues to assist in advancing the Kingdom's agenda.

Apostle Gray holds both a Bachelor's and Associate Degree in Theology and in May of 2016, he obtained his Master of Divinity Degree from Virginia Union Seminary in Richmond, VA.

Apostle Gray, under the unction of the Holy Spirit, began life Touch Ministries, a fellowship where he serves as a spiritual covering and mentor to senior pastors. He is happily married to his childhood sweetheart, the former Laverne Pressey. They have five children who serves alongside them in ministry.

Apostle Grays' desire is to see God's people live wholesomely, love much, laugh often and trust God with all their hearts.

Learn More About The Author

ApostleJohnGray.com
BethelRestoration.com

Grace4Purposeco.com

Made in the USA
Columbia, SC
18 June 2022